The Foundation Stage At Home

Helping Children To Achieve

The Early Learning Goals

A practical guide for parents and other carers to the education of children aged two to five years.

By Dr Shirley Cobbold

Published in Somerset, England, by SEC Publications (2019)

Table of Contents

Introduction

Who is this book for?

This book is principally for parents and other carers at home but may also be useful for professional childminders.

Early years education does not just happen while children are at school or pre-school. Young children are learning all the time and everything that they learn becomes part of their 'education'. It is impossible to turn off this learning process or to timetable it to only occur at certain hours of the day.

Since 2007 the Early Years Foundation Stage has applied to children in England aged from birth until they complete the Reception Year of primary school. Most children will be five years old at this point, although some will have quite recently turned five (summer birthday children) and others will be nearly six. The main focus of this book is the education of children during the three years before the end of the Foundation Stage: i.e. children aged two to five years. Outside England, the other countries of the United Kingdom each have their own versions of a Foundation Stage or Early Years curriculum. Each country is slightly different.

What is in this book?

This book answers the following questions:

- What is the Foundation Stage of education?
- Why is it important?
- What do children need to learn?

- How can parents and other carers support children's learning at home by taking account of the principles and content of the Foundation Stage curriculum?

The book describes the areas of learning that make up the Foundation Stage of education and explains the Early Learning Goals that are the expected outcomes when the Foundation Stage comes to an end.

How does this book help children to make a good start to their education?

When children start pre-school or school they will be following the Early Years Foundation Stage curriculum. Although the word 'curriculum' seems rather a grand term to apply to the educational framework for such young children, it remains the best word to describe the teaching and learning framework as it is enshrined in English law. However, a great deal of children's learning takes place at home. The Foundation Stage curriculum is a pathway towards a wide range of learning outcomes covering personal, social and emotional development, speaking, listening, literacy, mathematics and physical development, together with first steps in geography, history, science, technology, art and design. It is a curriculum, but, as this book aims to explain, it is one in which parents and other carers can be fully involved.

Parents who understand what children are being taught and how they are being taught are in a strong position to support learning at home.

What is The Early Years Foundation Stage

A brief history of the Foundation Stage

The Foundation Stage of education was introduced into all English schools in September 2000. The 2000 Foundation Stage curriculum was specifically for children aged 3-5 years. It comprised six areas of learning which were: personal, social and emotional development; communication language and literacy; mathematics; knowledge and understanding of the world; physical development; creative development.

In 2007 the Foundation Stage was merged with the Birth to Three Matters framework and was officially renamed the Early Years Foundation Stage. This was a framework for development and learning for children aged from birth to the end of the first year of primary school, which is known as the Reception Year.

In 2012 the areas of learning were reconstructed to put greater emphasis on three 'prime areas' and four 'specific areas', each of which is described and explained later in this book.

Also, in 2012 the number of Early Learning Goals was reduced from 69 to 17. Although this sounds dramatic, in fact each of the 17 new Early Learning Goals has several elements, so in practice the change was not that great.

For September 2014 a few more minor changes were made to the framework. The changes were mainly focussed on early years educational settings and childminders and included improving safeguarding requirements, and clarifying requirements for staff training

The current curriculum for the Foundation Stage?

The word 'curriculum' is easily misunderstood, especially in relation to the Foundation Stage. During the time that the curriculum was being developed there was a fear that children might be forced into a formal, restrictive style of education that would not be appropriate for their age. However, in most educational settings, the Foundation Stage curriculum has turned out to be flexible and child-focussed, recognising that young children learn best through playing, talking, exploring and investigating.

Parents and carers who read this book will gain an understanding of what the Foundation Stage curriculum means in terms of the day to day experiences of children. The statutory guidance for the Foundation Stage curriculum describes the characteristics of effective teaching and learning as ensuring that children have opportunities to:

play and explore

be involved in active learning

have opportunities to be creative and to think critically.

The Areas of Learning

The Early Years Foundation Stage curriculum is based on three prime areas of learning, aiming to promote all aspects of a child's development from birth to age five. These three areas of learning are:

Communication and language

Physical development

Personal, social and emotional development.

These three areas are fundamental to child development from birth onwards. As children make progress from about age two or three, the curriculum in some aspects becomes more geared to preparation for later academic learning (doesn't that sound grand?) and so there are four more areas of learning called 'specific' areas. These are:

Literacy

Mathematics

Understanding the world (I often wish I could do this!)

Expressive arts and design.

In each 'prime' and 'specific' area of learning parents and carers play a major part in helping children to learn through every day-to-day interaction and every planned or unplanned event. I know I keep saying this but children are always learning. They can't stop. But they can (and frequently do) learn things that are actually unhelpful to the development of their full potential. For example, some children quickly learn the advantages of having a tantrum in a supermarket or other public place They might even earn a 'reward' to keep their public behaviour on the straight and narrow! Another example (and I could write a long list of these) is that a child quickly learns that when one carer says no, a different carer might JUST say yes. Be reassured that this rapid learning is a sign of a good intelligence. But are you smarter than your two-year-old? Because you'll need to be!

A great deal of good quality learning can take place when adults join in with children's play, or when children join in with adults' everyday activities, such as shopping, cooking, writing or going for walks. Each of the areas of learning is discussed in much more detail later in this book. To provide more structure to the curriculum, within each area of learning there are Early Learning Goals. The Early Learning Goals are the targets that children will hopefully achieve by the end of their Reception Year in school.

The Early Learning Goals

The Early Learning Goals describe the knowledge, understanding, skills and attitudes that children are expected to have developed by the end of the Foundation Stage so that they are ready for the next stage (Key Stage 1) by the September after their fifth birthday. All of the Early Learning Goals are listed and explained in this book.

The Foundation Stage Philosophy

The 'philosophy' of education underpins decisions about what children should learn, why they should learn it and how they should learn it. The philosophy of the Foundation Stage curriculum emphasises that learning for young children should be centred on activities that are fun, interesting and motivating.

Early years experts know that if children are forced into 'formal' learning too soon they might decide that they do not want to learn anymore because they do not enjoy it. When the Foundation Stage was first introduced the government listened to the advice of early years experts and published guidance on how children should be taught. It stated that:

"Learning for young children is a rewarding and enjoyable experience in which they explore, investigate, discover, create, practise, rehearse, repeat, revise and consolidate their developing knowledge, skills understanding and attitudes. During the Foundation Stage, many of these aspects of learning are brought together effectively through playing and talking."

During all of the Foundation Stage, including during the Reception Year in primary school, an observer would be likely to see children doing the following things:

- Having fun
- Talking about all the things they do and think
- Making friends and learning to share
- Frequently making decisions
- Learning to be independent
- Being involved in many different activities
- Frequently choosing their own activities
- Sometimes working with an adult who directs the activity
- Learning both indoors and outdoors
- Frequently playing with adults who help them to learn
- Helping to make a mess and helping to tidy up.

Equality and inclusion

An important principle of Foundation Stage education is that educational activities should be designed to meet the needs of individual children. The words equality and inclusion are frequently used in official documents and sometimes cause confusion.

Equality does not necessarily mean that all children should have the same learning experiences. Rather, it means that activities should be designed to meet the learning needs of each individual child so that every child has an equal opportunity to learn and develop to their full potential. For example, if Jane is very confident and competent and needs greater learning challenges, she may well be involved in different learning activities from Mary, who is lacking in confidence and needs activities at which she can be successful more quickly. The learning needs of individual children can change very quickly as they develop.

Parents and carers should always aim to build on the existing knowledge, skills and understanding of individual children, leading each one towards the Early Learning Goals in small, manageable steps.

The curriculum guidance for the Foundation Stage states that no child should be disadvantaged or excluded because of their gender, race, colour, level of ability or home background. Adults should treat all children with respect and children should be learning to value and respect others. It is important that caring adults look out for, and respond to, occasions where children accidentally or deliberately try to exclude others from specific activities. Such actions can spring from innocence, but parents and carers should take time to explain how hurtful such behaviour can be.

When you plan activities for or with your children, aim to include each of the areas of learning regularly. It is important that children have a balanced education in the early years. Although children show natural preferences for some activities rather than others, they should not grow up believing that certain activities are only for certain people.

Here are some examples of the beliefs that some children and parents mistakenly have:

- That girls are not as good as boys at making things with construction materials.
- That boys do not enjoy stories, reading and writing.

- That playing aggressively is appropriate for boys because 'boys will be boys'.
- That children with physical impairments cannot join in with any physical activities.
- That children with sensory impairments (such as those associated with hearing or vision) cannot learn as quickly as other children.
- That children with a learning disability are not worthy of friendship.
- That certain races, cultures or religions are not worthy of respect.

Please be prepared to challenge these beliefs if you encounter them.

Sometimes it is necessary to gently persuade children to become interested in activities that they are not naturally drawn towards. Frequently, this can be done by imaginative planning. For example, writing activities can be developed within role-play. Wizards might be encouraged to write 'spells' and Bob the Builder would certainly need to write bills for his customers. Art and craft activities can be made more interesting if they are stimulated by an event that is of special interest to a child, such as a birthday or a visit to a special place.

Children have different favourite activities, but they all need equal opportunities to learn across all the areas of learning.

Assessment

There is often talk in the media about young children having to do tests. For example, we are told that there should be tests for children when they start school, or at the end of the Foundation Stage.

If, as a parent, you come across any one in a Foundation Stage setting who plans to sit your child down to do a test, particularly if it involves a pencil and a piece of paper be very wary indeed. Most experts agree that at Foundation

Stage children should not be expected to take tests. However, children are continually assessed. There is often a misunderstanding between the terms test and assessment. Teachers do assessments but this isn't the same as children doing tests.

The type of assessment that all Foundation Stage practitioners are trained to do is called Assessment for Learning and is based on careful observation. Practitioners will be keeping a close eye on what children like to do, what they are good at, what activities they might be avoiding or might need more practice at. Children should then be gently guided in the direction of developing their knowledge, skills and understanding. These on-going assessments will relate to all areas of learning and will always take careful account of what is developmentally appropriate for each child. These days, Foundation Stage practitioners are carefully trained to understand the normal developmental pathways towards the Early Learning Goals. The philosophy is that, through careful observation, practitioners will know where each child is on any specific learning pathway so that he or she can be encouraged to make progress to the next step.

The gap between what children can already do, or already know, and their next learning target should be small and manageable with an awareness that children will be learning at different speeds in different aspects of learning.

This process is one that most parents will already be familiar with. For example, when children first start to feed themselves they usually start with using their fingers, or a spoon. Later they will progress to using a knife and fork. And when a child is first starting to learn to ride a bike, the bike may be fitted with stabilisers, which are later removed. As parents you will be able to think of many similar ways in which you use Assessment For Learning at home.

The Foundation Stage Profile

At the end of the Reception Year at primary school, your child's teacher will compile a 'profile' that shows your child's level of attainment at that point in time. This is not a time for testing to see what each child can do, but a time for using all the knowledge that has been gained about each child to provide information about each child's current attainment in relation to the Early Learning Goals. The profile is based on the many hours of observation that school staff have undertaken over the course of the year when your child's progress towards the goals will have been regularly recorded. The end of the Foundation stage is a time to celebrate all the rapid learning and development that has taken place since your little tot was born. It is truly astounding how much children are able to learn and how quickly they are able to learn it.

The most up-to-date guidance on the Early Years Profile at the present time (2019) states that "practitioners' assessments are primarily based on observing a child's daily activities and events. In particular, practitioners should note the learning that a child demonstrates spontaneously, independently and consistently in a range of contexts."

Communication and Language

Communication and language is one of the three 'prime' areas of learning at the Foundation Stage. The official guidance for the Foundation Stage states that:

> "Communication and language development involves giving children opportunities to experience a rich language environment; to develop their confidence and skills in expressing themselves; and to speak and listen in a range of situations"

This area of learning is divided into three elements, which are:

- Listening and attention
- Understanding
- Speaking

For each of these elements there is a series of statements which describe the expected learning outcomes for each child. These individual learning statements are the Early Learning Goals. They are listed and explained below.

Learning Goals for Communication and Language

Element 1: Listening and attention

- ❖ Children listen attentively in a range of situations.
- ❖ They listen to stories, accurately anticipating key events and respond to what they hear with relevant comments, questions or actions.
- ❖ They give their attention to what others say and respond appropriately, while engaged in another activity.

13

Element 2: Understanding

- ❖ Children follow instructions involving several ideas or actions.
- ❖ They answer 'how' and 'why' questions about their experiences and in response to stories or events.

Element 3: Speaking

- ❖ Children express themselves effectively, showing awareness of listeners' needs.
- ❖ They use past, present and future forms accurately when talking about events that have happened or are to happen in the future.
- ❖ They develop their own narratives and explanations by connecting ideas or events.

Remember that the goal statements indicate what children are expected to be able to do at the end of the Foundation Stage. This sentence is repeated in each chapter because it is so important. Children are not expected to reach these goals until they are finishing their Reception Year. Of course, some children will achieve some of the goals earlier but parents are advised not to view children's progress as a race or a competition. Also, be very aware that at the end of the reception year some children will be only just five years old, while others will be nearly six years old.

During the Foundation Stage, one of the first priorities is to encourage children to speak clearly and to use language efficiently and confidently. As children develop their speaking skills they can use words and, in due course, conversation, to help them to make sense of all the interesting things that they see, hear, and experience.

The developing use of language is a very, very important aspect of learning for children during the Foundation Stage. Other areas of learning depend to a large extent on children's ability to listen and to express their ideas. Early years educationalists often comment that first children learn to talk but thereafter they talk to learn.

Communicating

Communication with children should be a two way process. Talking AT a child does not significantly promote learning. And just listening without responding is also an easy option that undervalues what children have to say. It is talking WITH a child, with meaningful two-way sharing of thoughts and ideas that strongly promotes learning.

So, to encourage children to communicate well it is important that adults take the time to listen to children. By listening carefully you will get to know a great deal about what your child thinks and understands. If you would like to develop your skill in promoting learning through communication, take time to listen to other adults and children talking and try to analyse exactly what is happening. Is it really a meaningful conversation that promotes the child's self-expression and understanding? It's noticeable that some adults find it difficult to listen to children and this is particularly true when a group of children all require adult attention.

If you are brave, record ten minutes of your conversation with a child and analyse what you record. For example:

- How many times do you speak?
- How many times does your child speak?
- How many words are in your child's longest sentence?
- Who leads the conversation?
- Do you ask questions to encourage your child to talk and think?

- When you ask questions, do you give your child enough time to think and respond?

You may be surprised at what you hear when you play the recording back!

Developing vocabulary

Remember that a two or three-year-old child may have no concept of what a word is. From the child's point of view, the language that they hear only has gaps when the adult stops speaking or pauses for breath. For example, when you use phrases such as 'It's time for bed', a young child will not realise that there are individual words within the phrase and this understanding can take some time to develop.

Encourage children to speak clearly and slowly and to develop their vocabulary. Aim to introduce new words each day and encourage children to ask the meaning of any word or phrase that they do not understand.

Tempting though it is, try to avoid copying your child's 'baby talk'. There is no need to correct mistakes; simply model the correct way to use words. For example, if your child says 'I putted my toys away', respond with something like 'You put your toys away. Thank you'.

Books and stories

When children listen to stories, or share non-fiction books with adults, there is a rapid improvement in language. As adults read to children they are likely to model slower and more correct use of language than they would use in everyday speech. This helps children to appreciate how sentences are constructed. Their own sentences will then gradually become clearer, longer and more complex. Through both stories and non-fiction books children can be introduced to new vocabulary and phrases that they might not normally hear.

Singing and reciting

Learning to sing songs or recite rhymes is also a valuable learning activity for Foundation Stage children. They generally enjoy experiencing pitch, rhythm and rhyme and as they sing or recite they develop clarity of speech and, most importantly, a more efficient verbal memory.

A leisurely visit to your local library should be a valuable learning experience for your children. Very young children might choose books according to the picture on the front cover, but gradually they can be encouraged to learn about different types of books and stories so that they can make more informed choices. The library is a place for sharing stories as well as choosing books to take home. There is always likely to be a comfortable seating area for an adult and a child to share a book

The power of imagination

Children frequently use language to organise their thoughts and actions. They do this when they are alone as well as when they are with others.

You may notice your child talking to himself or herself when they are involved in solitary creative activities, such as imaginary role play (when they pretend to be someone else - or even several other people all at the same time), small world play with models or 'play people', or art activities such as painting or modelling.

Do not feel that you should intervene at such times. When children use language to express thoughts or ideas to themselves, they are involved in a valuable learning activity. As well as developing language, your child is developing independence, concentration and perseverance.

Socialising

It is very important that children have the opportunity to talk with other children of a similar age. Children who have only limited opportunities to talk with other children can find peer to peer social relationships difficult when such socialisation becomes necessary. Socialising with other children generally demands better listening and negotiating skills than the child needs when socialising with adults.

Language is made of sounds

Children's awareness of words, and of the sounds within words, is strongly linked to later reading and spelling ability. As children start to use language, they begin to realise that sentences can be broken down into words. This realisation happens more quickly when adults encourage children to speak clearly by modelling clear speech themselves.

After awareness of words within sentences, children gradually become aware of sounds within words. Parents can encourage this awareness by involving children in word games and by encouraging familiarity with rhythm and rhyme through stories, songs and nursery rhymes. From about three years of age children become aware that some words rhyme and that longer words have rhythms provided by the syllables. Most children enjoy 'chanting games' with strong rhythm and rhyme. These are even more fun when they are combined with actions. There will be books and stories in your local library with nursery rhymes (traditional and modern), action rhymes and stories that have a strong emphasis on rhythm and rhyme. All of these are particularly valuable for shared reading

This early awareness of words and of syllables and rhymes is fundamental to reading success as your child progresses towards learning to read. This is because the 'phonic approach' to reading and spelling (more on this later) relies on an awareness of sounds in words.

Reading readiness

The Early Learning Goals for Communication and Language are sometimes classified as pre-reading skills, because the skills needed for learning to read, spell and compose writing are all embedded in language and communication. There is much more in this book about children learning to read and write in the section on Literacy, which you will recall is one of the three specific areas of learning.

Learning to enjoy books

With adult help, children will learn to enjoy reading before they are expected to learn to read. Learning to read is easier when the child understands that reading is fun. If you doubt this, think of your own past learning experiences. Would you want to learn to swim if you disliked being in the water? Would you want be an expert gardener if you disliked being outside in all weathers? Enjoyment and motivation are the keys to successful learning at all ages.

It's always best to share books in a quiet and comfortable place so that you can both enjoy a good story or discuss interesting pictures. Time is always a problem for busy parents, but this can be a relaxing time for all. It is important for male carers to share books with children too so that young boys do not start to view reading as something that men don't do.

You will notice the emphasis on sharing books rather than just reading stories. As you share the book, take time to discuss the story. What has happened? What will happen next? How do the characters behave? How do they feel? Some children greatly prefer factual books to stories so encourage children to make choices and express preferences and opinions. However, if you really feel that you cannot cope with the book about dinosaurs for the seventh time in a week, explain how you feel and ask to be forgiven!

Physical Development

Physical development is one of the three 'prime' areas of learning at the Foundation Stage. The official guidance for the Foundation Stage states that:

> "Physical development involves providing opportunities for young children to be active and interactive and to develop their co-ordination, control and movement. Children must also be helped to understand the importance of physical activity and to make healthy choices in relation to food."

This area of learning is divided into two elements which are:

- Moving and handling
- Health and self-care

For each of these elements the Early Learning Goals are listed below.

Learning Goals for Physical Development

Element 1: Moving and handling

- ❖ Children show good control and co-ordination in large and small movements.
- ❖ They move confidently in a range of ways, safely negotiating space.
- ❖ They handle equipment and tools effectively, including pencils for writing.

Element 2: Health and self-care

- ❖ Children know the importance of good health, of physical exercise and a healthy diet and talk about ways to keep healthy and safe.

❖ They manage their own basic hygiene and personal needs successfully, including dressing and going to the toilet independently.

Remember, as always, that the goal statements indicate what most children should be able to do at the end of the Foundation Stage when they are between five and six years old.

In the past, it was sometimes the case that educational settings gave this area of learning a low priority. This was unfortunate because it is a very important aspect of children's development. Young children are usually full of boundless energy, but energetic periods can be followed by sudden and extreme tiredness. Adults need to be alert to the signs and prepared to modify plans and routines to fit in with children's 'rhythms'. Encouraging a tired child to be interested in your most exciting new idea this week is probably a waste of your time. The exciting activity can wait until the child is ready. Likewise, it is not a good idea to attempt to focus a child on a sedentary activity that requires a high level of concentration if he or she is full of energy that needs to be released into physical activity. This can cause frustration for both adult and child.

Strength, stamina and coordination

The lifestyles of many children allow far less opportunity for physical activity than in past times. Lack of physical activity can have adverse effects on children's health, co-ordination and cognitive ability.

Physical skills need to be developed at both the 'whole body' level (sometimes called gross motor skills) and at the finer level of hand to eye co-ordination (sometimes called fine motor skills). 'Whole body' control and co-ordination is an important developmental step towards the finer motor skills needed for tasks such as drawing and writing. Children who lack opportunities to develop strength and stamina when they are young can fall into a habit of lethargy. This means that, as they get older, they will be reluctant to become involved in the sort of activities that they might have enjoyed spontaneously when they were younger. Consequently, there is an impact on health and fitness in the longer term as well as in the short term.

Exploring outdoor spaces

To achieve the Early Learning Goals children need space to run, stretch and play. Most homes have limited indoor space but gardens, local parks, playgrounds and leisure centres can provide excellent opportunities for developing whole body physical co-ordination. If you have a garden, do not begrudge it to your children. It is true that plants and shrubs may get accidentally damaged, but they will regrow. Encourage outdoor play in all weather. As long as children are wearing appropriate clothes, the weather should not be a problem. Invite friends' children over and let the children play!

In cold weather children need loose, lightweight, warm layers of clothes. In hot sunny weather they need to be well protected with loose cotton clothes that protect their skin from sunburn. Children will need some protection with sun cream but current advice appears to be that some natural sunlight on skin is beneficial.

Activity Ideas

When children have space, most will show a natural inclination to run. Such free and spontaneous exercise, in a safe place, is both natural and beneficial.

Where space is a bit more limited, or when you want to structure children's exercise, consider encouraging activities such as:

- obstacle courses
- mini sports day activities
- mini football matches
- mini cricket matches
- mini tennis or badminton tournaments
- dancing.

The children will soon start organising their own activities once you have given them a lead.

Developing the challenges

When children are involved in physical activities, be prepared to intervene at appropriate times to develop and improve skills and provide increased challenges for children who seem ready. Children's levels of confidence vary tremendously. Some children will need continual support and reassurance in order to develop their confidence and skill, but others will need encouragement to slow down and become more controlled. As always, adults need to be responsive to the learning needs of individual children.

Activity Ideas

For throwing and catching, use soft items such as foam balls or beanbags while children are developing their confidence. This will ensure that they are not deterred from taking part because they are frightened of being hurt. If a hard item, such as a football, is thrown towards a child it can be frightening if the child does not know how to catch it.

Soft, household items such as pillowcases stuffed with old clothes or scarves tied into loose knots can be used as alternatives to bought items. Larger items are easier to catch than smaller items. Throwing, kicking or rolling balls towards targets will develop awareness of space and hand to eye co-ordination. Singing and dancing games, from disco dancing to country dancing, are valuable for developing awareness of space in relation to other people or objects.

Learning about how to keep healthy

From an early age, children need to learn that healthy eating and exercise are important. They may not believe that eating their crusts will make their hair curl (well did you believe it?) but they will probably understand that their bodies need good food for fuel in the same way that cars and buses need good fuel in order to keep working correctly.

Children are naturally very interested in their own bodies. They like to feel their muscles working and their heart beating and they are interested in what bones thy have and what their lungs are for. They are more likely to be able to understand that healthy eating and plenty of exercise lead to strong muscles and bones if they have some understanding of what muscles and bones are, and what they do. After physical activity, children will tell you about the effects of exercise when they say, 'I'm out of breath', 'I'm hot', or 'I'm thirsty', so there should be plenty of opportunity to draw their attention to the causes of how they feel. Because they are always interested in how their bodies work, they like to learn about what it is inside them that is causing their heartbeat, or what is happening inside when they breathe heavily.

Making use of household items

There is a range of equipment that a pre-school or school might have, but which not all homes will have, such as balls, beanbags, hoops, tunnels, mini-trampolines, climbing frames, slides or swings. However, much equipment can be created from odds and ends. For example:

- A rolled-up pair of socks can be a 'beanbag';
- An old hat can be a 'Frisbee';
- Garden canes balanced on flower pots can make safe hurdles for jumping over or crawling under;
- Skipping ropes placed in parallel lines on the lawn can become a 'river' to jump over;
- A single skipping rope at ground level can be a 'tightrope' to balance along;
- Plastic bottles filled with water can become skittles to be knocked down;
- A bucket, bowl or hoop placed on the ground makes a good target to throw things into;
- An old bucket with the base removed can be firmly attached to a house wall or tree so that children can play 'basketball'.

Be creative!

Also, as previously mentioned, do not forget to make use of the facilities at your local park or leisure centre.

Using tools and materials

Children use tools and materials during all sorts of activities but art or craft activities are particularly valuable for developing early physical skills. From the earliest finger painting to the more advanced forms of designing and making there are many opportunities to help children develop the skills that, in due course, lead to the level of hand and eye co-ordination that is required for writing. Also, children develop physical co-ordination through many day-to-day activities as you encourage them to be independent. Skills such as doing up buttons or zips are everyday occurrences for independent children.

In physical development, as in all other aspects of development, children progress at different speeds. If you overestimate what your child is capable of, you are likely to make unreasonable demands.

For example, it has been a traditional expectation that young children should learn to 'tie up their own shoelaces' but this is described by experts as 'one of the most complex motor and perceptual skill operations a human ever learns' (Woodfield, 2004). Thank goodness for Velcro!

Writing as a physical skill

Writing with a pencil is also a physically demanding skill and adults often underestimate how difficult this is for a child. Do not rush your child into trying to write letters. The hand to eye co-ordination and the level of concentration required for this is quite advanced.

To develop co-ordination and control, involve your child in activities such as drawing, colouring, tracing, painting, modelling or constructing. In fact, any activity that encourages children to co-ordinate their hands and eyes is valuable. In the Foundation Stage curriculum writing is also listed within the 'specific' areas of learning, so there is much more about the process of learning to write later on in this book. Writing is a very complex set of inter-related skills and the physical challenge of holding and manipulating a pencil is just one of many components. The physical control and co-ordination required to draw and trace should be mastered before children are required to learn correct letter formation. Otherwise frustration will set in. As one four-year-old tot cried out in despair as he threw the pencil on the floor…….. **"I can't do it!!"**

And he was quite right. He couldn't do it because he hadn't been taken through the correct learning process to prepare him for learning to write.

Keeping children safe

Parents and carers need to make continuous and careful decisions regarding children's safety. Young children obviously have to be kept safe, but as they grow older they should start to learn how to assess risks for themselves. We need to talk with children about strategies for staying safe and assessing risk, but at the same time we don't want to make them unduly nervous. If we protect our children too carefully they may not have the sort of challenging experiences that enable them to take care of their own personal safety in the future.

For example, children who never have the opportunity to run or roll down grassy slopes will not learn to gauge how fast they can go and remain safe. They will not learn how to stop, or how much space they need to stop. Children who never have the opportunity to climb trees will never learn to tell a safe manoeuvre from a dangerous one. The challenge for caring adults is to encourage adventure, but with careful supervision, and to involve children in discussions about safety issues as soon as they are old enough.

Take time to encourage your child to handle tools and objects correctly and safely. Each new skill learned is transferable to other similar situations.

Discuss the consequences of taking risks and, where you have any doubts about children's ability to be safe, ensure careful supervision.

For less closely supervised moments, use only tools that you know are safe. For example, in an unsupervised activity, do not let children use items that can cause suffocation, be put in ears or up noses, or which have sharp points or edges. Children (like adults) become safer when they are healthily aware of danger and have developed skill in assessing and managing risk.

Personal, Social and Emotional Development

Personal, Social and Emotional Development is one of the three 'prime' areas of learning at the Foundation Stage. The official guidance for the Foundation Stage states that:

> "Personal, social and emotional development involves helping children to develop a positive sense of themselves, and others; to form positive relationships and develop respect for others; to develop social skills and learn how to manage their feelings; to understand appropriate behaviour in groups; and to have confidence in their own abilities."

The area of learning is divided into three elements. These are:

- Making relationships
- Self-confidence and self-awareness
- Managing feelings and behaviour

For each of these elements there is a series of statements which describe the expected learning outcomes for each child.

On the following pages, these individual learning statements, i.e. the expected outcomes of the Foundation Stage of education are listed and explained. Be aware that the statements indicate what children are expected to be able to do at the end of the Foundation Stage, when they are ready to move on to Key Stage One. Children will progress through various stages of learning as they move towards attaining the goals. It is a gradual process of learning and developing.

The Foundation Stage is the only phase of education that puts personal, social and emotional development as one of the highest priorities for learning. Many educationalists would argue that it is the most important of the areas of learning, not just for the Foundation Stage, but for all other stages of learning as well. In adult life 'good interpersonal skills' are highly valued.

Learning Goals for Personal Social and Emotional Development

Element 1: Self-confidence and self-awareness

- ❖ Children are confident to try new activities and say why they like some activities more than others.

- ❖ They are confident to speak in a familiar group, will talk about their ideas, and will choose the resources they need for their chosen activities.

- ❖ They say when they do or don't need help.

Element 2: Managing feelings and behaviour

- ❖ Children talk about how they and others show feelings; they talk about their own and others' behaviour and its consequences and know that some behaviour is unacceptable.

- ❖ They work as part of a group or class and understand and follow the rules.

- ❖ They adjust their behaviour to different situations and take changes of routine in their stride.

Element 3: Making relationships

- ❖ Children play co-operatively, taking turns with others.

- ❖ They take account of one another's ideas about how to organise their activity.

- ❖ They show sensitivity to others' needs and feelings and form positive relationships with adults and other children.

The Early Learning Goals for Personal and Social Development remind us of how the achievement of the goals is a very gradual process. To explain this, consider what you might see at a party arranged for children aged between two and three years. Many parents will constantly feel a need to intervene, either to protect their more sensitive and shy children from being upset or to ensure that their exuberant and assertive children are not causing havoc to the extent that they might never be invited to a party again. We do not expect that younger Foundation Stage children will have the same knowledge skills and understanding as children who are a few years older. If ever we have underestimated the importance of early years education, and having targets to work towards, that children's party will convince us that there is a lot for children to learn.

The process of supporting and encouraging learning is often called 'scaffolding' in psychological terms. An adult provides the scaffold that enables learning steps to be taken, with scaffolding that is no longer needed (because the step has been achieved) being taken away and new scaffolding being designed to help children progress to the next step. Most good parents are doing this all the time even without thinking about it, but being aware of it makes decisions about how to react to behavioural issues much easier. In contrast, we have probably all seen examples of bad parenting where such scaffolding is absent. Such examples would be where parents ignore children's over-assertive behaviour or where they comment disparagingly to others about children's abilities within earshot of the child. And we have all been amazed at what children hear when we think they're not listening!

Children's personal, social and emotional development is influenced by all that they see and hear. Therefore, all adults who have contact with children should be expected to set good examples. In particular, they should model good manners and show respect for all children and adults. They should stay calm, rational and consistent, even in difficult situations such as when children become fractious. It isn't easy, but it is important.

So, what should parents do to promote those Early Learning Goals when things are not going too well? The first thing is not to panic. Try not to respond impulsively when you perceive a huge gap between your child's present level of attainment and the goal that you aspire to on their behalf. Think constructively and make a plan. Be your own 'Agony Aunt'.

Here are some practical examples relating to the Personal, Social and Emotional area of learning.

Dear Agony Aunt, My three year old wants to join in with our family board games, but she spoils every game. For example, in snakes and ladders she won't take turns and she gets upset when she lands on a snake and has to go down. Family games have become a nightmare but we don't want to exclude her. What shall I do?

Response from AA:

Celebrate that your child has a drive to be successful. Carefully channelled this will be a bonus in later life.

Choose your games carefully. For example, snakes and ladders presents two challenges. First the challenge of taking turns and then the problem of going down the snakes.

To tackle the taking turns issue, for about a month play (or oversee) games with your child where only two people need to take turns so that the waiting time is not too long. After a month, progress to games with three people.

At the same time talk to your child about the 'taking turns' process and why it is important.

Encourage your child to talk to you when they feel cross and frustrated. This is called 'emotional literacy' and is a very important part of personal, social and emotional development.

Obviously, we can't all have an Agony Aunt for every stressful situation (sorry, I should have said every learning opportunity) so parents need to either be their own AA or, even better, work with a group of friends or family to develop their strategies. Incidentally, the process above provides 'psychological scaffolding' towards the achievement of part of an Early Learning Goal. It's just an example of good parenting really. The same good practice should be delivered by the trained practitioners in your child's Foundation Stage setting.

There are a few specific points within this set of early learning goals that are worthy of particular mention: These are:

Children will "choose the resources they need for their chosen activities"; It is really important that children have freedom to do this. It doesn't mean that they can choose from the entire toy catalogue or even that they can choose from the entire contents of their toy cupboard, but the message is that parents are advised not to be too controlling. If your child is creating a picture or collage, remember who the artist is.

Children will "say when they do or don't need help". Independence is valuable, but so, realistically, is time if you are getting ready to go to pre-school that unfortunately starts promptly at 9.00. Here the message for parents is, whenever possible, to offer help rather than insist on helping. If you have to insist on helping, then explain why you have to help while you are doing it.

Children "adjust their behaviour to different situations". Children are often experts at doing this as you might find out when you talk to your child's first teacher and think that the child they are describing is so perfect it can't possibly be yours. Naturally, children learn to take advantage of the fact that you love them. If they have a turmoil of negative emotions that they need to express they will obviously do that in the safest environment. Sometimes you have to just roll with the punches (hopefully not literally though). Talk with your child soon afterwards to try to find out what caused the turmoil and to help her or him to deal with their annoyance more constructively. But don't underestimate the time and effort that this takes. Did anyone ever say that parenting was easy? Well for some lucky parents it is, but not for all parents all of the time. Remember to appreciate the joy on the good days and remember to TELL your child how much you appreciate them when everything is going well.

Learning to enjoy learning

At the Foundation Stage, children's motivation to learn is just as important as their ability to learn. At this vital early stage of education, interest, excitement and developing confidence provide the bedrock of learning. Children will be excited about learning if adults are excited and enthusiastic about the shared activities. So try to involve your child in activities that you both find stimulating and enjoyable and keep looking for new things to do.

As you have conversations with your child about what they are doing, be prepared to do more listening than talking.

Developing concentration

Although adult involvement is an essential part of children's learning, there will be many times when your child becomes deeply involved in activities that they have chosen themselves. If you notice your child concentrating deeply on a solitary task, such as 'reading' a book, making a model, or exploring in the garden . . . tiptoe past. Don't interrupt. At that point you are not needed and the skills of concentration that your child is developing are an important factor in all learning. Make the most of the quiet time and put the kettle on. Your little treasure will soon be back, bombarding you with ideas or questions, probably before you have had time to drink your tea!

Self-identity and self-esteem

Between the ages of two and five years, children are learning a great deal about who they are and the similarities and differences between themselves and other children. This is a time when children need to be assured that they are valued and valuable. The development of confidence and self-esteem is strongly influenced by adult and child interactions from babyhood onwards. If the relationships between adults and children do not support this learning, a consequent lack of confidence and self-esteem can develop quickly and last for a very long time. However, if you have a child who is particularly shy or timid or, at the other end of the spectrum, particularly extrovert and noisy, don't feel that this is necessarily all caused by interactions with adults during the formative years. Studies of twins has shown that even identical siblings brought up in the same way in the same environment by the same people can be very different from each other in terms of personality and confidence. A very old adage regarding early years teaching is that all planning for learning should 'start from the child'. That is where all educational learning journeys must start. On any journey, it's just not helpful to say that you know where you want to go but you don't want to start from where you currently are. Help to develop children's self-esteem by showing that you value the sort of people they are despite the occasional 'blips'.

Emotional literacy

Emotional literacy is concerned with encouraging people (children and adults) to recognise, understand and talk about their feelings and needs. Most young children experience strong emotions and show their feelings readily. Parents of older children recall their memories of the 'terrible twos' with a shudder. However, by the age of three years, most children are starting to gain some control over their emotions and are entering the 'age of reasoning'. Remember that children vary considerably in all aspects of their development and emotional development, in particular, is a very gradual process. With your help, your child's understanding of feelings such as joy, sorrow, anger, frustration, happiness and wonder will develop as they progress through the Foundation Stage.

Emotional literacy and language development

Emotional literacy is strongly linked to the ability to express thoughts and ideas in words. As soon as children are able, encourage them to talk about their own feelings. Adults can help young children to be aware of feelings such as happiness, sadness and anger through everyday conversations, through stories and through role-play. It is no secret that one of the reasons for those terrible two tantrums is that children are too young to use language to express their emotions in any other way. Wouldn't it be great if your two-year-old had skill in negotiation and compromise?

"Well actually Dad, I really don't want to have my lunch at the moment? Unless you want to have to drag me to the table kicking and screaming I need a bit more time to put these plastic bricks together to make a car. If you give me more time to fix my car I'll eat my lunch especially quickly. OK?"

(Dream on, Daddy!)

As children get older, they will learn to understand that their feelings cause them to behave in certain ways. As children learn to make sense of their feelings, and understand how their feelings affect their behaviour, they are likely to become more considerate of the feelings and behaviour of others. It is not a good idea to try to reason or negotiate with a child who is very angry or frustrated. It is more helpful to calmly repeat a consistent message, such as, 'We will talk about it when you stop being cross.' When the tempest is over, try to get your child to explain what caused it.

Activity Ideas

Looking at photographs of people's faces can provide an opportunity to help children understand the range of emotions that they might feel themselves. Drawing and painting are also activities that can provide a focus for discussion about children's feelings and the feelings of others.

Children can learn a great deal about how to care for others by sharing responsibility for a family pet. They will appreciate that pets have needs that must be met. Because such animals are dependent on humans, children can be encouraged to understand that it would be cruel to ignore needs such as the need for food and water, the need to be taken for a walk, or simply the need to be loved.

Children need experience of being loved, respected and cared for so that they are able to learn to love, respect and care for others. Therefore, make sure that children are familiar with the rules of polite and respectful behaviour by modelling them yourself. Children learn a great deal through imitation. Of course they don't always copy your impeccable behaviour, but if they don't have polite and respectful behaviour to copy they stand no chance of learning it. It is particularly important that children are encouraged to have respect for people who might be perceived as 'different'. As they gradually meet more people, they will appreciate that although people are different in some ways, they are also similar in many ways.

Learning to socialise

Young children need opportunities to socialise with adults and children from outside their home circle, so be prepared to create opportunities for your child to make regular contact with different groups of people. It is surprising how often parents are not aware that their children are nervous of unfamiliar places and faces until the day that they first take them to a pre-school group or to school. It is unfair to expect a child to be confident in a new situation if he or she has had little experience of such occasions. Inviting other children and their carers into your home is an excellent starting point. Your child can then start to form friendships in a familiar and secure environment. The obvious next step is to return the visit. Talk to your child about the visits and about the process of making friends.

Learning to share

Most very young children have a natural reluctance to share their possessions, and they frequently seem to class their favourite people as possessions that they do not want to share. Learning to share, like learning to take turns, has to be taught gradually. It develops in tandem with a growing awareness of the feelings of others.

Expectations of behaviour

Even before children are able to communicate with language they are starting to learn, from the body language of their nearest adults, what they are allowed to do and what they are not allowed to do. Try to be clear in your own mind about what sort of behaviour you want to encourage and discourage. If a child has several carers, it is important that consistent messages are given.

You might think that adults agree about what 'good' behaviour looks like, but in fact adults can have widely different views on this. Children are quickly confused if they receive different messages and are understandably likely to get cross if they are allowed to do something between (for example) 9 a.m. and noon, but not allowed to do it between noon and bedtime.

Think about how you make your child aware of what is good behaviour and what is not acceptable. Remember to reward good behaviour. This is so important and often forgotten. Rewards for good behaviour must be something that your child enjoys or values; if possible, something that they have chosen themselves. Although it is a bit old fashioned, mini reward systems such as stars or marbles in a jar can work well. Small rewards can be accumulated by the child to be exchanged for a bigger reward when enough of the mini rewards have been accumulated. It has been argued that such reward systems can encourage a materialistic approach to life, or that they could be interpreted as a bribe to behave nicely. But hey! Sometimes we all need a bit of extra incentive. Parents must make their own decisions about what is appropriate for each child, but the power of praise is often underestimated. Above all, be consistent with whatever scheme you implement. Young children react strongly when they perceive something to be 'not fair', even before they fully understand the concept. From a child's perspective it can be 'unfair' when caring adults have differing expectations of behaviour.

It is important that parents and carers think carefully about how they convey the message that certain types of behaviour are unacceptable. Remember that punishments do not have to be something unpleasant, they can simply be the withholding of a reward that would follow good behaviour. Shouting at a child is not a good strategy for changing behaviour. Even if it deters bad behaviour in the short-term, your child will soon become immune. Also in the longer term it will cause different problems because children learn such a lot through imitation. Shouting is best only used in an emergency situation if a child is about to do something dangerous. In other situations it is just a form of verbal aggression.

Learning personal independence

Although it is often tempting to do things for your child because it is quicker or tidier, resist it if you can. Allow him or her to enjoy the sense of achievement from having put on their own shoes and coat even if the shoes are on the wrong feet and the coat is on upside down! Eventually they will ask for help if the shoes start to hurt or the hood of the coat gets in the way. Of course, if their health or safety is an issue you will have to tactfully intervene, but the general rule is to encourage independence.

Making choices and active learning

Formal schooling puts an emphasis on adult-directed activities, but the Foundation Stage curriculum requires children to have plenty of opportunity to select activities and organise themselves. If you still have a picture in your mind of Foundation Stage children sitting at desks completing endless worksheets, banish it now. The Foundation Stage is play based and active. Children should be learning through using their senses, through movement and with increasing use of language. They learn best through doing, thinking, talking and (of course) having fun.

Literacy

Literacy is one of the four 'specific' areas of learning at the Foundation Stage. The official guidance for the Foundation Stage states that:

> "Literacy development involves encouraging children to link sounds and letters and to begin to read and write. Children must be given access to a wide range of reading material (books, poems and other written material) to ignite their interest."

This area of learning is divided into two elements, which are:

- Reading
- Writing

For each of these elements the Early Learning Goals are listed below.

The Learning Goals for Literacy

Element 1: Reading

- ❖ Children read and understand simple sentences.
- ❖ They use phonic knowledge to decode regular words and read them aloud accurately. They also read some common irregular words.
- ❖ They demonstrate understanding when talking with others about what they have read.

Element 2: Writing

- ❖ Children use their phonic knowledge to write words in ways that match their spoken sounds. They also write some common irregular words.

❖ They write simple sentences which can be read by themselves and others. Some words are spelt correctly and others are phonetically plausible.

Learning to read and write are two very complex processes. Although reading and spelling are strongly linked, there are other aspects of writing, such as the physical elements and the composing elements that are discrete skills. Each skill has its own 'learning journey'.

Research shows that there are no long-term benefits in teaching children to read and write at a very young age. Children who are taught formal literacy skills later generally learn faster and have more positive attitudes to reading and writing.

Other aspects of literacy that you have read about in previous chapters, such as understanding and enjoying books and developing hand to eye co-ordination are important pre-reading and pre-writing activities. In due course, children will begin to develop skills in writing and spelling. As stated in a previous chapter, it is important to remember that the physical skills needed to keep a pencil line under control take a long time to develop. Therefore, resist the temptation to start to teach your child to read and write before they are fully prepared. The Foundation Stage of education aims to prepare children for later success. To be clear on this, it isn't a question of passively waiting for children to become 'ready' for reading and writing, as was a philosophy during the 1960s. It's about making sure that the early levels of knowledge, understanding and skill are carefully developed with all children so that 'failure' does not occur.

I can read!

Most children go through a period of 'pretend reading' where they point to the text and make up the story. They may even have memorised the story and therefore appear to be reading the words. As you observe closely you may notice that the child is not actually pointing to the words that they are speaking! Do not discourage this phase or tell your child that they are 'not really reading', as this might destroy their pleasure in books and stories.

As children learn more about words, letters and letter sounds they will realise for themselves the difference between reading words and 'telling a story'.

The alphabet and letter sounds

When it comes to learning about the alphabet, there has been debate in the past about whether children should be taught letter sounds, or letter names, or both. Politicians have been particularly keen to have a say in this debate! Knowledge of letter sounds is more helpful to children when they start to read and spell. Learning letter sounds and letter names at the same time can lead to verbal memory overload. For example, if you tell children the names and sounds of all the letters of the alphabet and also tell them that some letters make more than one sound and some sounds are represented by more than one letter, expect them to be confused and lose interest. This would be information overload! Knowledge of the most common sounds made by a few letters is all they need to know to start with. Scaffold your child's learning. (See Chapter 4.)

Old-fashioned games such as 'I Spy' can encourage children to pay attention to the sounds at the beginning of words and this can be done without any formal teaching and without learning to recognise the letters of the alphabet.

Learning to recognise alphabet letters can come later as it relies heavily on visual and verbal memory. Make sure that word games are not too difficult. Many four-year-olds will have difficulty finding something beginning with the sound 'b' when a wide range of objects is available, but will, for example, be able to choose an animal whose name begins with the sound 'b' when looking at three models or pictures of a snake, a bear and a cat.

When children are experienced at identifying sounds and rhymes in words they can gradually be introduced to the sounds associated with each letter of the alphabet. But initially, is the understanding of the link between sounds and letters that is most important. The actual knowledge of which sounds link to each letter can be developed over time. As children learn letter sounds, do not encourage them to say sounds with a long 'uh' at the end. For example the word 'dog' begins with the 'd' sound and not with a 'duh' sound. Likewise, 'snake' begins with 'sss' and not 'suh' and 'mouse' begins with 'mmm' and not 'muh'. If the pure forms of the sounds are used, later blending of sounds to make words (which is so important when reading) will be easier.

Phonic fun

As children progress through the Foundation Stage they can be encouraged to start to combine their gradually developing knowledge of sounds in words with their gradually developing knowledge of the sounds and shapes of the letters of the alphabet. In the jargon of the school classroom this is often called 'learning phonics'. Building on the carefully constructed knowledge and understanding that they have (with your help) developed, they will start to read and spell words 'phonetically'. This means that they will attempt to read a word by sounding out the letters and attempt to spell a word by breaking it down into sounds. At a later stage your child will learn about the irregularities of English spelling. For the moment, allow them to enjoy their newly discovered ability to read and spell some words.

Don't destroy a child's sense of achievement by insisting on a level of perfection that they are not ready for. This is acknowledged in the Early Learning Goals when it states that children are expected to "use their phonic knowledge to write words in ways that match their spoken sounds". For example, "I sor a don ce on the beech" is a very good attempt at 'phonetically plausible spelling' for a child aged five years.

Decoding print and recognising words

There will come a time when Foundation Stage children are able to match some spoken words with the corresponding printed words. For many children the word that they recognise first is their name. Learning to match the printed word to the spoken word is much easier for children who are able to match letter sounds with letters, because they can use the letters as 'clues' and start to blend the sounds to help them to read the word. This is called decoding in the jargon of the Foundation Stage.

Children who can decode find it easier to read words that have a good match between the individual letter sounds and the sound of the word as a whole. For example, it is easy (with practice) to blend the sounds of 'c', 'a' and 't' into the word 'cat', but impossible to blend the sounds 'c' 'o' and 'w' into the word 'cow'. Words that do not follow the main phonic roles are often called irregular words. In some classrooms they are called 'tricky words'. Children also find it easier to learn to read words that are nouns, such as 'Jane', 'dog' or 'house' than more abstract words, such as 'the', 'was' or 'went'. There are many enjoyable activities that can encourage children to learn to match written words with spoken words. For example, lotto games where children need to match words with pictures can be bought or made.

If you are making activities to help children to recognise written words, make sure that your writing is clear and that letters are formed correctly. For example, make sure that the letter 'b' does not look like the numeral '6', and that the letters 'o' and 'a' do not have gaps at the top. Use lower case letters except for so called 'proper nouns', such as people's names or the names of places: i.e. not peter or PETER but Peter.

Some children learn to read words from story and non-fiction books quite easily, although in fact this is quite an advanced skill. Do not expect too much of your child too soon. Learning to read early does not necessarily make children better readers in the longer term and children who are pressurised into learning early sometimes lose motivation very soon.

Writing: A shared experience

In relation to early writing skills, the first stage of learning is for the child to understand that writing conveys messages. Adults can demonstrate this to children by sharing their writing activities. For example, explain what you are doing as you write a shopping list, write a letter or even send a text. Modelling writing at a computer can also be included here.

Writing: A creative activity

Because children learn such a lot through imitation, they are likely to start to copy your writing activities. They will make 'letter-like squiggles' and tell you 'what it says'. This understanding of writing and the desire to write are very important stages.

As children start to learn the sounds and shapes of letters and gain awareness of sounds in words they will start to be aware of the differences between their 'letter-like squiggles' and the letter shapes that they see during their daily activities. This would be an appropriate time to start to raise awareness that there is a 'correct' way to write letters. However, be sensitive. Do not risk destroying your child's pleasure in writing to communicate meaning by demanding a level of hand control or spelling that is beyond their capability.

Writing in role-play

Early writing can be fun when it is part of role-play. If your child loves to dress up as a 'doctor', encourage her to play at writing prescriptions, or bedside notes. If your child likes to dress up as a 'shopkeeper', encourage him to pretend to write orders or bills. Remember that as a play partner YOU can model the reasons why writing is useful. Don't expect children's writing to look like yours!

Handwriting: Learning to drive the pencil

And here is yet another reminder that the physical skill in learning to control a pencil line is very difficult indeed. As scaffolding, parents can help children to learn to draw normal size letters by first giving them practice of drawing letters on a larger scale. For example, finger painting is great for tracing large letter shapes and your garden patio or decking could be an ideal place for drawing letters with jumbo chalks. If this is a step too far for garden proud parents, then ropes or scarves could be used to create letter shapes so that children can 'do the letter walk'. All such activities can develop awareness of the 'route' that a pencil will eventually need to travel to draw a letter.

At a more advanced stage, the triangular 'pencil grips' sold in early learning shops or stationery shops are helpful for encouraging children to hold a pencil or crayon correctly. It is not an easy thing to do when you first try! The advantage of developing a correct pencil grip at an early age is that it helps to develop a neat, relaxed and fast writing style later. Correct letter formation leads a child easily into a flowing, cursive (joined up) writing style in due course.

When your child reaches this stage, highlighter pens are useful to write messages that a child can trace over. Allow your child to choose the words and sentences to write so that she or he has ownership of the meaning of the writing. Your child then becomes the composer of the writing and the owner of the message. Parents and carers will need to learn to write their letters clearly using lower case letters except (for example) to begin people's names. When children are ready to learn to write in a more formal sense, as they make the transition from 'play writing' to real writing', they will need to become aware that there is a correct way to form each letter.

Books that show correct letter formation are available in high street stores. But buy the book to teach yourself how to form each letter correctly so that you can explain and model correct letter formation for your child. Don't rush your child into this stage of writing. If you do so, you run the risk of creating a writing phobia!

If you have access to a tablet computer there are some good apps that can be used to help children to form letters correctly. However as always with apps, there are more badly designed ones than good ones. One good example is Hairy Letters for iPad.

Mathematics

Mathematics is one of the four 'specific' areas of learning at the Foundation Stage. The official guidance for the Foundation Stage states that:

> "Mathematics involves providing children with opportunities to develop and improve their skills in counting, understanding and using numbers, calculating simple addition and subtraction problems and describing shapes, spaces and measures."

This area of learning is divided into two elements, which are:

- Numbers
- Shape, space and measures.

For each of these elements the Early Learning Goals are listed below.

The Learning Goals for Mathematics

Element 1: Numbers

- ❖ Children count reliably with numbers from 1 to 20, place them in order and say which is one more or one less than a given number.
- ❖ Using quantities and objects they add and subtract two single-digit numbers and count on or back to find the answer.
- ❖ They solve problems, including doubling, halving and sharing.

Element 2: Shape, space and measures

- ❖ Children use everyday language to talk about size, weight, capacity, position, distance, time and money to compare quantities and objects and to solve problems.
- ❖ They recognise, create and describe patterns.

❖ They explore characteristics of everyday objects and shapes and use mathematical language to describe them.

Remember, as always, that the goals indicate what children are expected to be able to do at the end of the Foundation Stage. In the specific areas of Mathematics and Literacy in particular, the gap between what a three-year-old child can do and what a five year old child is expected to be able to do can seem enormous. Don't panic! You will be amazed how quickly they can learn. From an early age children can be helped to become aware that mathematics is all around them. Mathematical vocabulary, which includes numbers, the names of shapes and the language of measurement and position can be introduced naturally during many day-to-day activities.

Surprisingly often, adults feel negative about mathematics after having had bad experiences at school. Some parents think of mathematics as being all about signs and symbols. If you feel like this about mathematics, try to make sure that your children do not grow up feeling the same way. It is really a very practical subject and, at the Foundation Stage, signs and symbols do not really need to be used at all because it is the understanding of mathematics that is important.

Try to use every possible opportunity to develop children's understanding of mathematics and mathematical language. For example:

Children can be encouraged to notice numbers on clocks, shapes on buildings and symmetry on butterflies.

Their attention can be drawn to how coins are used to buy and sell items.

They can learn about counting as they help with domestic chores, such as putting socks into pairs or counting out mugs for each person to have a drink.

Understanding what numbers mean

One of the difficulties when starting to teach mathematics is that children can learn to count without developing any real understanding of numbers. This occurs when they are taught to count by rote without being taught to associate the words that they are using with the actual process and purpose of counting. Teachers in primary schools can always tell when this has happened. The conversation goes something like this:

TEACHER: (Showing Jane three model animals in the model farm) How many animals are in the 'field', Jane?

JANE: 1,2,3,4,5 (Without any attempt to touch or count the objects)

TEACHER: What lovely counting. So how many animals are there?
JANE: 1,2,3,4,5 (This will be the end of the conversation as far as Jane is concerned.)

Jane 'can count', but she has no understanding of the meaning or purpose of what she is doing. So, the message is to count and talk about numbers in a meaningful way whenever an opportunity occurs. You will soon notice that such opportunities occur very often when you start to look out for them.

Activity ideas

To make counting meaningful, count with a purpose with your child at every opportunity. For example:

- count together as you go up and down stairs
- count together as you do up the buttons on clothes

- count together as you put the tins of baked beans into the shopping trolley. Have you got enough tins? If there is one tin in the cupboard at home, how many will you have altogether?

Furthermore, don't just count together but also talk about counting together. Encourage children to think about why we need to count. With your help, they will come to understand that counting is a useful skill in practical situations.

Counting accurately

Children also need to be helped to count accurately. When they first learn to count they find it difficult to co-ordinate their verbal counting with the number of objects that they are counting. They should be encouraged to touch or move items as they count them, but even then you will find that they might count 'accurately' up to five as they touch or move four objects. Or they might count up to four as they touch or move five objects. This shows a lack of understanding of the 'one to one' nature of counting and is a natural phase.

With more experience of counting for different purposes, children gradually develop the skill of counting accurately.

Recognising numerals

A numeral is a symbol that represents a number. For example '3' is a numeral. Children are often fascinated by numerals, particularly numerals that are special to themselves, such as their age, the number of their house, or how many days it is until a special event. Adults can build on children's interests by drawing their attention to numerals during everyday activities.

Don't be afraid to talk about big numbers in general terms, but also focus on helping children to learn to recognise the numerals 0 – 9.

Activity

Make, borrow or buy a board game for your child that uses a dice (such as the traditional snakes and ladders game). The best dice are those on which you can write the numerals, then rub them off and change them day by day. For example, younger children might play a game just using numbers 1, 2 and 3, with each numeral drawn twice so that all six faces of the dice are used. Older children could use numbers 1-6 in the traditional way.

When talking about numbers, don't forget the number nought! It is a very important number that is associated with a very important concept. In due course, children will understand that it means 'no objects' and to realise that nought is fewer than one.

Understanding the 'conservation of number'

An important milestone in children's mathematical development occurs when they show understanding that the number of objects in a group stays the same if the objects move their position. In classroom jargon this is called understanding the 'conservation of number'. A younger child will feel that it is necessary to recount the objects after they have been moved to see how many there are. However, a more experienced child will know without counting that the number of objects is the same if none have been added or taken away.

Activity

An interesting experiment is to put a row of objects on the table and ask a child how many there are. When the child has counted accurately and told you how many there are, make the row of items longer by spacing them out. As you do this make sure that the child can see that you have not taken any away or added any. Then ask the child again how many objects there are. When the child can tell you the correct number without recounting, you will know that he or she understands 'conservation of number'.

Drawing numerals

Many children have difficulty when it comes to drawing numerals. The physical co-ordination needed to draw numerals, as with writing letters, is frequently underestimated. It is as hard as first learning to drive in straight lines and around curves!

Comparing numbers

Although the Early Learning Goals require children to 'add, subtract and share', this is not necessarily about the traditional process of 'doing sums'. Doing sums (like counting) can be done with an incomplete understanding of addition, subtraction or division. So, what can parents and carers do to promote understanding? Make the most of everyday opportunities to use words and phrases such as: 'more than', 'fewer than', 'less than', 'most', 'fewest', 'a lot', 'not many', 'the same number as'. As children get older and their understanding of this language seems firm, start to build on this by introducing more advanced language such as: 'one more than' and 'one fewer than' Some people feel more comfortable with the word 'less' instead of 'fewer', although fewer is generally considered to be grammatically correct. The idea of sharing items in a numerical way is also one that can be introduced to children through everyday activities. Do you remember doing . . . "one for you, one for me, one for you, one for me" as a child?

And when sharing a single object the concept of fractions can be developed quite naturally in language terms. Can the pizza be cut in half to share between two people? Are the two halves the same size? Is half a pizza too big for one person? Maybe each half should be cut in half again so that three people can each have a quarter? How many quarters will be left? Wow! What a lot of maths! And all we planned to do was have some lunch.

Matching one to one

In order to understand the concepts of more and less, children need to be able to match items 'one to one', just as they have to match the objects to the spoken numbers when they are counting. Your child will be able to see how many more (or fewer) there are in one group of objects than another group of objects when he or she has matched, one to one, the items from one group with the items in the second group.

For example, if you have invited visitors to your house, involve your child in a discussion about what you need to prepare. How many cups will you need if all the adults want coffee? How many glasses will you need if all the children want juice? How many people will there be altogether? Have you got enough biscuits for everyone or do you need more? If there are not enough biscuits for each person to have one, how many more will you need to get? If there are more biscuits than people, how many people can have two?

In practical situations, such as the one described above, children will often concentrate long and hard on solving mathematical problems.

Number songs and number rhymes

Number songs and number rhymes are very useful to develop children's understanding of addition and subtraction. For example, songs such as 'Five

Little Ducks Went Swimming One Day' help children to 'see' the subtraction process as, at each verse of the song, one duck 'does not come back'. At the end of the song the ducks can all swim back together or they can swim back one by one. Your local library will have books and DVDs that contain similar songs and rhymes.

Number line games and board games

Games using 'number lines' can be used to help children to understand number, calculate and recognise numerals. For example, numeral cards can be pegged onto a 'washing line' using clothes pegs. The imaginative use of a character (such as a mischievous teddy) to mix up or hide certain numbers will motivate children to find the missing cards and put the numerals back in the right order.

Board games using dice provide opportunities to develop many mathematical skills, such as recognising numerals and counting forwards and backwards. However, bear in mind that younger Foundation Stage children may not have the patience to play games in which they have to wait for a turn, or the social skills to cope with not being the winner. For such children, games will need to be designed to take account of their levels of maturity. In games with older children, the levels of challenge can be varied by changing the information on the dice, or by using more than one dice. For example, a dice could be made with the faces showing: +1, +2, +3, -1, -2, -3. This would help children to understand the relationship between addition and counting forwards, and subtraction and counting backwards. Using two dice, the children could have to add numbers together to find out how many spaces they could move on the board.

Learning mathematics through practical, day-to-day activities

It is very important that children learn their mathematics through practical activities. All too often in primary schools, children are expected to learn about measuring and weighing by comparing pictures of objects. So, during practical activities with real objects, introduce your child to mathematical ideas and language such as light and heavy, short and long, small and tall, full, half-full and empty, faster and slower, wider and narrower, fatter and thinner.

Encourage children to use language correctly when comparing objects. Many children compare objects using incorrect phrases such as 'bigger an' or heavier an' instead of 'bigger than' and 'heavier than'.

Shapes and patterns

Children are often naturally observant of shapes and patterns in the environment and their interest can be used as a starting point for discussions and questions. For example: Why are doors rectangles? Why are butterflies symmetrical? Why are wheels circles? You do not have to know the answers to the questions. Trust the children to give you some interesting ideas… and then to give you some even more challenging questions!

Children are not expected to know the mathematical names of all shapes at the Foundation Stage, but they will quickly learn the names of common shapes as part of normal language development and they can be helped to notice the differences between shapes. Through their play activities they will start to learn that square shapes can be difficult to push through round holes and that some shapes are better for a particular purpose. It is easier to build tall towers with cubes and cuboids than with spheres and pyramids!

Positional language

Learning to describe 'position' is, as always with mathematics, all to do with using language correctly. Look for opportunities to explore opposites in practical situations, such as under and over a bridge, in front of and behind the tree, or inside and outside the house. How many more can you think of?

Indoor or outdoor games such as the old favourite 'hide and seek' can be an excellent way to developing children's understanding of positional language. Will they know that they are learning to understand important mathematical concepts?

The BIG message is: Make maths fun and make maths meaningful.

Activity Ideas

Try to present your child with mathematically challenging questions. Here are some ideas.

- How can we measure how much it rains in one week?
- How can we find out which of these cuddly toys is the heaviest?
- How can we find out which of these cuddly toys is the fattest?
- Have we got enough flour and sugar to make this cake? How many eggs do we need?
- How many minutes does it take to walk home from playgroup?

Understanding The World

Understanding the World is one of the four 'specific' areas of learning at the Foundation Stage. The official guidance for the Foundation Stage states that:

"Understanding the world involves guiding children to make sense of their physical world and their community through opportunities to explore, observe and find out about people, places, technology and the environment."

This area of learning is divided into three elements, which are:

- People and communities
- The world
- Technology

For each of these elements the Early Learning Goals are listed below.

The Learning Goals for Understanding The World

Element 1: People and communities

- ❖ Children talk about past and present events in their own lives and in the lives of family members.
- ❖ They know that other children don't always enjoy the same things, and are sensitive to this.
- ❖ They know about similarities and differences between themselves and others, and among families, communities and traditions.

Element 2: The world

- ❖ Children know about similarities and differences in relation to places, objects, materials and living things.

❖ They talk about the features of their own immediate environment and how environments might vary from one another.

❖ They make observations of animals and plants and explain why some things occur, and talk about changes.

Element 3: Technology

❖ Children recognise that a range of technology is used in places such as homes and schools.

❖ They select and use technology for particular purposes.

Within this diverse area of learning there are the first steps of knowledge and understanding relating to several traditional school subjects. For example, within the first element there are links to history and religious or cultural studies and within the second element we can see the early stages of the science and geography curricula for Key Stage 1, which is the phase of education that follows the Foundation Stage.

Past and present

During in the Foundation Stage, children will gradually develop an understanding of the passing of time. As language develops, children often show confusion about words such as 'yesterday', 'tomorrow', 'last week' or 'next year'. Even at age four words such as 'before' and 'after' will frequently be used incorrectly. Adults often assume that children have an understanding of such vocabulary, when in fact they have not. Some children become quite skilled at asking questions that will help them to gauge time. For example:

- Will it be tomorrow when I wake up?
- How many sleeps until my birthday?
- Are we nearly there yet?

The best way to help children to develop a sense of time is to bring the vocabulary into day-to-day conversations whenever you can.

At age four and five, although it may be too early for a proper history curriculum an understanding of some of the differences between past and present times is often of interest to young children.

Activity ideas

Visits to local places of historical interest, such as castles and old houses, can provide children with stimulating first-hand experiences. Some tourist attractions now go to considerable lengths to try to re-create past times realistically.

Stories and non-fiction books can also be used to engage children's interest, particularly if they are related to the sorts of visits mentioned above.

Conversations about people and occasions that are important to individual children will obviously be of greatest interest, and the memories of grandparents are invaluable for comparing past and present ways of life. Children are often fascinated in how people lived in the 'olden days'.

Outdoor science

Never underestimate how much scientific learning can take place in a garden or local park. Most children have a naturally strong interest in science and scientific investigation. It is an element of learning that provides endless opportunities to explore and investigate, both indoors and out.

Activity ideas

Children can have a wonderful time in the garden as they hunt for mini-beasts, finding out where the animals like to live and what they like to eat.

They can go out and blow bubbles on a windy day, investigating how fast the bubbles will float away in sudden gusts of wind.

In winter, they can investigate ice and snow. Look at the patterns made by the frost and ice. How does snow feel when you hold it in your hands?

In spring they might be able to watch tadpoles change into frogs, or chicks hatch out of eggs, or even lambs being born.

In summer warmth they can investigate the characteristics of water and water pressure as they play with tubes, funnels and squeezy bottles.

If children are taken on good old-fashioned nature walks, they can observe and investigate the effect of the changing seasons on animal and plant life.

Indoor Science

Activity ideas

Children can investigate what happens when colours are mixed as they explore paints, or coloured water, or torches with coloured film.

They can explore how sound travels by attaching tin cans to each end of a long piece of string and making 'walkie talkies'.

They can investigate magnetism with magnets, large paper clips and other interesting objects.

They can explore how food ingredients change as they are mixed and then cooked.

They can plant seeds in tubs and learn about germination and growth.

They can explore the effect of pumping air into little stretchy containers (balloons).

And what should parents and carers do as all of this exciting scientific learning is going on? They can enjoy introducing children to the many aspects of the environment that adults are usually too busy to notice. They can learn to see the world through children's eyes again. Children will ask questions as long as they know that you will listen. Do not worry if you do not know all the answers. Say when you don't know and find out together. It's all fun!

A sense of place

This goal will later become the Key Stage 1 subject of geography, but this does not mean that children should learn about places far away. Try to take children out and about in the local neighbourhood as much as possible.

During visits to the shops, park, supermarket or leisure centre, or on visits to friends and relatives by car or public transport, encourage children to discuss what they see. Children also enjoy reliving enjoyable experiences through role-play, or through small-world play with miniature people or puppets.

Older children can be encouraged to make comparisons between different places. For example, children may have interesting views on questions such as:

- Is it better to be on the beach or at the swimming pool?
- Is it better to live in a house, a bungalow, a flat or a caravan?
- Is it better to travel in a car, or a train, or a bus, or to walk?
- Why do people spoil places by leaving litter and who should pick it up?
- What are rivers for?

- . What is the difference between a big hill and a mountain?

Different cultures and beliefs

Where children live in multicultural communities, there are frequent opportunities to learn from others about the traditions and festivals that are an important part of different cultures. In communities that are less multi-cultural, it is slightly more difficult for children to learn about the beliefs and traditions of others. However, with careful thought, it can be done. For example, children can learn that people do not all use the same language, eat the same food, wear the same clothes or attend the same churches. Books and carefully selected children's television programmes can develop children's knowledge and understanding. It is important to help children to understand that although there are some differences between people of different nationalities and cultures, there are also many similarities.

Technology

If there's one thing that grows and changes faster than young children it's technology! Children now accept technology as an integral part of their lives. Even three-year-olds seem to be able to use TV remote control devices without being taught. And in the Apple shop, which is not in the fruit market, there are special little tables and chairs so that young children can play on iPads. What amazing marketing!

Computers and programmable toys

If you love computers, tablets and programmable toys, that's great, but please encourage children to use them constructively for learning and then only for limited periods of time. It is debated whether prolonged use may cause harm such as eyestrain, but what does do harm is that children who spend too much time with techno devices (or indeed with television) are likely to be missing out on other experiences and learning, especially those that involve language, communication and physical activity.

Of the many programmable and electronic toys that are marketed directly at children through toy shops, there are many that are not suitable, for a variety of reasons. So make sure you try before you buy. Some 'speaking' toys use unfamiliar accents or digitised speech, making it difficult for young children to understand. Others aim to teach children inappropriate knowledge or skills, such as teaching letter names at a time that it would be more beneficial for them to learn letter sounds.

Using 'Apps'

In the last few years there has been a huge increase in the production of 'apps' for tablet computers that are specifically aimed at young learners, but again the quality is variable . Although these are often very cheap or even free for the annoyingly termed 'lite versions' again the message is try before you buy. Consider what your child is actually learning from the app and whether there is a better, more active way to learn it. Then carefully monitor your child's use of the tablet in terms of time and the learning that is taking place. There are some very good apps to help children learn to draw letters and learn letter sounds, but there is also a lot of rubbish being marketed as app makers get on the bandwagon. Talking story apps can be very attractive to young children and the quality is improving all the time. But should they replace visits to the library? And of course you can't have a cuddle with a tablet computer as the story is read.

Technology in the local environment

As you take your children out and about they will be able to see how technology is used in their everyday world. For example, how is technology used at the library, at the supermarket, at the bank, on a building site or on a farm? They will, of course take it entirely for granted and will be amazed to discover that their parents had to manage without it!

Expressive Arts And Design

Expressive arts and design is one of the four 'specific' areas of learning at the Foundation Stage. The official guidance for the Foundation Stage states that:

> "Expressive arts and design involves enabling children to explore and play with a wide range of media and materials, as well as providing opportunities and encouragement for sharing their thoughts ideas and feelings through a variety of activities in art, music, dance, role-play, design and technology."

This area of learning is divided into two elements, which are:

- Exploring and using media and materials
- Being imaginative

For each of these elements the Early Learning Goals are listed below.

The Learning Goals for Expressive Arts and Design

Element 1: Exploring and using media and materials

- ❖ Children sing songs, make music and dance, and experiment with ways of changing them.
- ❖ They safely use and explore a variety of materials, tools, and techniques, experimenting with colour, design, texture, form and function.

Element 2: Being imaginative

- ❖ Children use what they have learnt about media and materials in original ways, thinking about uses and purposes.
- ❖ They represent their own ideas, thoughts and feelings through design and technology, art, music, dance, role-play and stories.

Here is the last gentle reminder that the goals indicate what children are expected to be able to do at the END of the Foundation Stage. But in this specific area the reminder is really not necessary because babies, toddlers and older children all LOVE most aspects of art, music, dance and drama. Even if they are too young to join in they will respond with excitement to music and stare raptly as people dressed up as colourful and interesting characters strut their stuff on CBeeBies TV.

Valuing creativity

In the 2000 Foundation Stage curriculum this area of learning was called Creative Development, which is a much better and more comprehensive title.

The development of creativity is a very important aspiration for children of all ages and a strong argument can be made that there are links between creative capability and success in adult life. For example, in many careers there is a need for people who can be creative in solving problems or in designing improved products and services, not to mention scientific and technological research and development, which frequently requires creative thinking.

Despite this, there is sometimes a tendency to undervalue this area of learning in favour of other areas. The truth is that all of the Foundation Stage areas of learning are interrelated and interdependent and all should be equally valued. The popularity of television programmes that encourage us to be creative in our kitchens and gardens indicates that many of us aspire to be creative. Perhaps it is because creativity has often been mainly associated with leisure activities that is has become undervalued in schools. There is perhaps also a belief that creativity cannot be taught. Whatever your views on this, the Foundation Stage curriculum encourages us to promote and value children's creativity in a variety of different ways and in a variety of situations.

Children often re-create experiences through role-play and art, giving them an opportunity to remember and reflect on things that they have done. This reinforces the learning in memory. Children also use creative activity as a means of expressing emotions and learning to understand them. Creativity should be valued as a talent in its own right, not just as a means to an end. If children do not develop confidence in their ability to be creative, they may always be inhibited from achieving their potential.

Art and craft

Art and craft activities can be delightfully messy so parents need to think carefully about the right location for activities to take place. Children need access to materials and tools for activities such as drawing, colouring, painting, modelling and collage. Try to set activities in a meaningful context so that children are inspired to be creative. You might, for example, encourage children to create a picture about 'the weather' just after a thunderstorm, or model clay animals after a visit to a farm.

The main role of the adult is to encourage creativity by providing choices of materials and by valuing children's ideas. It is all too easy to stifle creativity by seeming to criticise or by ignoring children's achievements. Parents and carers must be aware that if a child is asked to copy something that has been created by someone else, they are not developing creative skills. Similarly 'colouring inside the lines' and 'painting by numbers' are not creative activities. As a parent, if you want to make a clay pink pig after the farm visit, go ahead and make one. Enjoy! But don't expect your child's animal to look exactly like yours. It is important that your child doesn't think that yours is 'right' and that his is inferior. To be creative, children need to have confidence in their decisions.

The role of the adult

Although the adult should not take over the role of decision maker in creative activities, children may welcome support with some of the physical skills involved, such as cutting things out or fastening things together. Where such help is needed but not given, children may become frustrated because their lack of physical dexterity holds them back from creating something that they have imagined. However, it is important also to encourage their independence in the physical skills in the longer term. As always, adults need to be sensitive to the individual needs of particular children.

In preparation for creative activities, you will find it useful to start a collection of attractive and useful everyday materials, such as coloured paper of different types, a variety of pens, pencils, crayons, paint brushes and rollers, fabrics, packaging materials and anything else that comes your way!

Make sure that children's clothes are well protected. Some types of glue and dark coloured paint can be very difficult to remove from clothing and children should not be inhibited by a fear of 'getting messy'. Old, adults' shirts, worn back to front, are ideal.

Don't forget that art is not necessarily an indoor activity. The 'great outdoors' provides plenty of scope for such things as collages and sculptures created with natural materials.

Pop, jazz, opera or CBeebies?

It is said that children will respond to music even before they are born and many parents report on the soothing properties of music for fractious babies.

Most adults enjoy music of some sort or another, although tastes differ. Sometimes we prefer a certain type of music because it is the sort we were 'brought up on'. It is valuable to introduce children to different types of music so that they can appreciate the great variety of forms of music that there are.

Creating and composing

Young children are fascinated by their ability to create sound. The activities that can encourage children to investigate sound are generally easy to organise in a home environment. There are many opportunities to make and explore sounds using a variety of different objects. Perhaps some readers can remember activities such as filling glass jars with varying amounts of water and tapping with a metal spoon to produce different notes, making 'guitars' with elastic bands or creating 'maracas' by filling containers with small stones, rice, sugar, or anything else that might make an interesting sound. Overheard, "Mummy, please can I use some frozen peas to make a maraca?"

If you have a piano, or other type of cherished instrument, it is tempting to ban little fingers from touching it. However, it is far more valuable to teach children, at an appropriate age, how to treat such instruments with respect and provide supervised opportunities for them to explore its potential.

Instruments designed specifically for children can also be great fun. Items such as tambourines, drums, maracas or xylophones might be available from your local toy library.

Singing together

For those readers who enjoy singing, sharing songs with children can be a joy in much the same way as sharing a good story. If you are thinking that

73

although you can sing you don't know any suitable songs, then CDs are readily and cheaply available in many high street shops, or probably from your local library. There is a good argument that CDs with just audio tracks have an advantage over DVDs which have both audio and video. This is because with an audio track the child has to focus more on the sound and listening skills are being developed.

Additionally, whilst listening to an audio track, a child can be involved in doing something else at the same time and is not staring passively at a screen. From age three years, most children will be able to join in with a few simple and familiar songs. By age five, many will be able sing some songs from memory with a fair degree of accuracy.

Moving to music

Children just LOVE moving to music. In fact they usually can't help it. Just play the music and watch them jiggle! This sort of natural and uninhibited response should be encouraged. Why not join in and jiggle too?

As children get older they can be helped to introduce more creativity and style into their response to music. This is when 'movement' starts to become 'dance'. Your child will be influenced by the types of dance that they see, so be prepared to enjoy your child's first attempts at ballet, Irish jigs or ballroom dancing.

Creative role-play and small world play

In role play children dress up as characters they would like to be and enact the role. In small world play they organise model characters and are quite capable of enacting a story in which they take on the role of every character in turn. If you've never REALLY watched children in this type of activity you have missed something very special. Sometimes just being an observer is priceless! Role-play and small world play are types of play that most children organise for themselves spontaneously. Sometimes they role-play alone but it can be a very social activity that strongly develops children's communication skills. Children will role-play at being all sorts of different characters. Adults who can involve themselves as play-partners, without becoming the decision makers, are worth their weight in gold. Overheard as child is talking to daddy: "No you can't be the Fairy Godfather this time because it's your turn to be the pumpkin":

Activity ideas

Children might:

Create tracks for their trains, or roadways for their cars and trucks.

Create environments in a sand tray for a dinosaur world, a play park or a building site.

Create miniature gardens using natural materials.

Design and make a boat for their pirate game using cardboard boxes.

Create a den in the garden from a garden table and some old sheets. This could become a treasure cave, a fairy grotto or a dragons den.

Compose a music symphony with their friends using a collection of children's instruments supplemented with saucepans and wooden spoons etc.

With very few 'props' (because children can make practically anything be practically anything) parts of your home could become: a doctors surgery, a dentists surgery, a vets surgery, a hospital, a shop, an airport, a café, a hairdressing salon or a garden centre.

Feel free to add to this list but if you wish to join in the play, remember not to be 'bossy'.

Designing and making

Some children might have a preference for designing and making in an 'arty' way with, for example, different types of paper, card or packaging materials, glue, paperclips or staples. Alternatively, they might prefer to be in the garden building with bricks and mortar, or wood, nails and a hammer. Remember that children using tools such as these must be supervised carefully.

Activities such as modelling with dough, plasticine or clay can also provide opportunities for children to explore the properties of different materials and use a variety of modelling tools.

Manufactured construction kits, such as Duplo and Meccano, can provide good opportunities to design and assemble. There are many such kits available but choose with care. Some kits provide only limited opportunities to create different models. Choose a kit that gives children scope to be imaginative. Avoid the temptation to make things for your child to copy. Also avoid any temptation to criticise what they create, although challenging questions such as 'Can we move it, do you think?' 'Will it fall over if the wind blows?' or 'Where shall we keep it?' are appropriate.

Combining creativity with communication skills

Parents can encourage children to talk about all of their creative activities by asking questions. Try to ask 'open' questions that expect a longer answer than just 'yes' or 'no'. This will develop children's language and thinking.

'Open' questions begin with words or phrases such as: Why? How?, Where? What? Can? For example:

- Can you tell me about?
- What does it do?
- What would happen if?
- What do you think?'

Allow children plenty of time to respond to your questions. There is always a temptation for adults to ask children questions and then to provide answers before the child has had time to form a response. A tradition amongst modern early years educators has been to use the ten second rule, where the questioner waits at least ten seconds after asking a question to allow a child to answer. Often it will take a young child that long to plan the reply with the words in the right order.

A Note for Professional Childminders

If you are a professional childminder, accountable to OfSTED, whenever you plan activities make sure that you have a sufficient knowledge of the Early Learning Goals to be able to articulate (both verbally and in writing if asked to do so) which goals the activity is likely to promote.

Then, when you carry out each activity with the children, make sure that you actually DO promote that learning by making sure your resources are suitable, by asking the right questions, by allowing enough time and by providing the appropriate levels of support for individual children.

At the end of the activity you should be able to articulate what you feel each child has learned, practised or otherwise gained from the activity and how the activity has contributed to each child's progress towards achieving the Early Learning Goals.

Professional childminders who can confidently do the above, will be using observational assessment to identify each child's next learning steps so that they can plan appropriately for the next day or the next week.

As well as assessing each child's progress through your careful observation, you should be routinely evaluating your own performance in preparing for, and carrying out, the activity. You should be able to articulate what went well and what needs to be improved for next time.

If you are able to do all of the above, whilst staying relaxed, cheerful and continually motivated by your commitment to children, you are a STAR and OfSTED should ask no more of you!

About The Book And The Author

I published the first edition of this book in 2002 when the Foundation Stage curriculum was still very new to parents and educationalists alike. I wrote it because I wanted to 'demystify' the curriculum and help parents understand that early years education still had its roots in good parenting.

Having worked with young children in educational settings for many years, I felt I had knowledge and experience that I could share. Following my years as an early years teacher, I became a teacher trainer and researcher at the University of Gloucestershire. I had a particular interest in the development of literacy skills and I was concerned that many practitioners lacked understanding of the developmental progression of reading and writing skill.

In 2006 I was invited by Nelson Thornes Publishers to create an extended version of my book that was more specifically aimed at accredited childminders who suddenly found that they had to follow the Foundation Stage curriculum and that OfSTED would be popping in every now and then to check that they were doing it correctly. A scary prospect!

In 2007 the Foundation Stage curriculum for children aged three to five years was combined with the development framework for Birth to Three Matters. When the two frameworks were combined the current Early Years Foundation Stage curriculum was created. This aimed to provide a progression map for the development and learning for children aged from birth to five years. Some would argue that when the two frameworks were combined it led to a 'watering down' of advice for each of the phases, rather than a well thought through integration of the two. At this time, because there were changes to the Early Learning Goals, my previously published books became outdated.

My books were never intended for a huge audience, as the guidance only applied to settings in England. Nevertheless, several thousand copies were sold, with local authorities and parenting groups sometimes ordering large numbers for distribution.

In 2012 the Early Years Foundation Stage curriculum was changed again. The number of Areas of Learning was increased and the number of Early Learning Goals was reduced. However, as each Early Learning Goal is now longer and more complex than previously, the actual content and coverage of the goals has changed very little.

This book is a revised edition of the first book that was published in 2002. It is aimed predominately at parents rather than childminders so does not contain the 2006 supplement that was specifically included to support accredited childminders, such as information about the OfSTED inspection framework.

It is a book for parents who love their children (as most of us do) and want the best for them. If at times it sounds a bit 'preachy' I apologise. Hopefully it contains some explanations and ideas that you might find useful. If you have read the book and learned nothing new, then congratulations! You are a great parent. I hope you enjoyed it anyway.

The 2014 edition of this book is currently only available as a Kindle version. The Kindle edition has the advantage that I was able to incorporate photographs and captions, which was great fun. Unfortunately, printing costs make this impossible with this Amazon generated paper version. I believe some older versions of the printed book are still available from online secondhand book shops, but of course the older versions are not fully up-to-date with the changes that have been made to the Early Learning Goals.

The Kindle version, with its colour photographs and captions is still available on Amazon and is fully up to date.

Thank you for purchasing this version of my book.

Printed in Great Britain
by Amazon